SNAKES SET I

KING COBRAS

Megan M. Gunderson
ABDO Publishing Company

visit us at
www.abdopublishing.com

Published by ABDO Publishing Company, 8000 West 78th Street, Edina, Minnesota
55439. Copyright © 2011 by Abdo Consulting Group, Inc. International copyrights
reserved in all countries. No part of this book may be reproduced in any form without
written permission from the publisher. The Checkerboard Library™ is a trademark and
logo of ABDO Publishing Company.

Printed in the United States of America, North Mankato, Minnesota.
042010
092010

 PRINTED ON RECYCLED PAPER

Cover Photo: Getty Images
Interior Photos: Alamy p. 9; Getty Images pp. 6–7, 8, 10–11, 19; Peter Arnold p. 21;
    Photo Researchers p. 15; Photolibrary pp. 4–5, 17

Editor: Tamara L. Britton
Art Direction & Cover Design: Neil Klinepier

Library of Congress Cataloging-in-Publication Data

Gunderson, Megan M., 1981-
  King cobras / Megan M. Gunderson.
     p. cm. -- (Snakes)
  Includes index.
  ISBN 978-1-61613-436-5
  1. King cobra--Juvenile literature. I. Title.
  QL666.O64G86 2011
  597.96'42--dc22
                                     2010013422

CONTENTS

KING COBRAS

What do you know about king cobras? Did you know they are the longest **venomous** snakes on Earth? In addition, cobras are vertebrates. When threatened, their skin stretches and their neck bones expand into a warning hood. Scales and sharp fangs help protect these powerful reptiles.

Cobras are cold-blooded creatures. That means the temperature of their surroundings affects their body temperature. So, cobras avoid extreme cold and heat. If they get too cold, their bodies won't work. If they get too hot, they will die.

King cobras belong to the family **Elapidae**. Coral snakes, mambas, and sea snakes belong to the same family. Yet king cobras belong to their own genus, *Ophiophagus*. The name means "snake eater." These kings rule over other snakes!

Another name for the king cobra is the hamadryad.

SIZES

Just how long are the longest **venomous** snakes on Earth? Most king cobras do not grow more than 12 feet (3.6 m) in length. However, the record length is 18 feet (5.6 m)!

There are a lot of muscles in all that length! These strong snakes can lift one-third of their bodies off the ground. That means the largest king cobras can appear taller than the average human!

Even raised up, king cobras are able to keep moving forward. That makes these slender creatures appear very threatening.

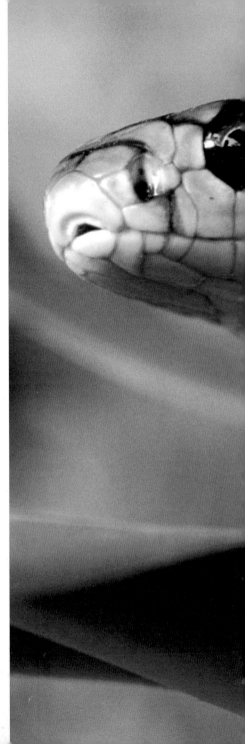

King cobras can weigh up to 20 pounds (9 kg).

COLORS

All king cobras do not
have the same body coloring.
Their appearance depends
partly on where they live.
Those that live in dark,
thick forests are generally
darker in color. King cobras
that live in open forests and
plains usually have lighter
bodies.

A king cobra's body can be
yellow brown, black brown, gray
green, or light olive. Some have
white, yellow, or beige bands

A snake's scales protect it from rough ground as well as prey that fights back!

across their backs. The cobra's belly is pale yellow. Its tail is dark olive to black.

Young king cobras are dark brown or black with yellow bars across the back. There are also yellow markings on the hood. Some still have these patterns as adults. On others, the bands fade with age.

WHERE THEY LIVE

King cobras are content in a variety of **habitats**. They are found in rain forests, bamboo stands, and mangrove swamps.

These snakes also enjoy open ground, such as agricultural areas and **plains**. King cobras will live in mountain regions, too. They are found up to 6,500 feet (2,000 m) above **sea level**.

Whatever their habitat, king cobras live mainly on the ground. Yet these fierce predators are also excellent climbers. King cobras will chase prey into trees! Swimming is easy for them, too.

King cobras often live near streams.

Where They Are Found

The king cobra's favorite **habitats** are all found in Asia. These snakes live as far west as India. King cobras are also found in the nearby countries of Bangladesh, Nepal, and Bhutan.

From there, the king cobra's range extends east into China. It also covers Laos, Thailand, Cambodia, and Vietnam. The king cobra calls Myanmar and Malaysia home, too.

These long, slender snakes aren't limited to the mainland. King cobras also live on islands. They are found in Brunei, Indonesia, and the Philippines.

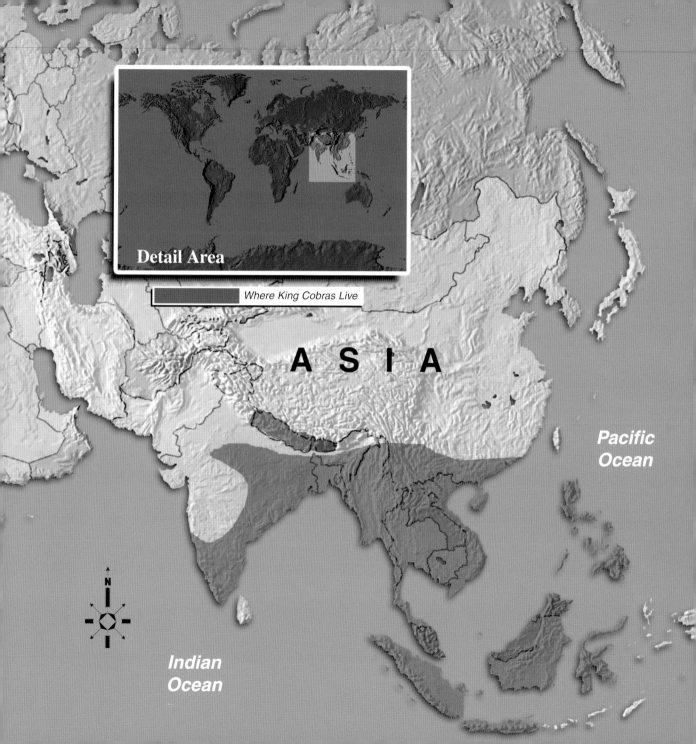

Detail Area

Where King Cobras Live

ASIA

Pacific
Ocean

Indian
Ocean

SENSES

King cobras have better eyesight than many other snakes. They can spot the tiniest movements! And, raising up their heads helps them see better.

You might think snakes can't hear, because they don't have **external** ears. But that isn't true! Cobras use their lower jaws to sense vibrations in the ground. The vibrations travel from their jawbones to their inner ears. In this way, they can sense predators and prey that wander by.

Like many animals, cobras smell through their nostrils and taste with their tongues. What makes snakes special is that their tongues also help them smell!

King cobras rely on their keen senses to explore their surroundings.

A cobra flicks out its forked tongue to pick up scent particles in the air. These enter the Jacobson's **organ** on the roof of the mouth. That organ determines exactly what those odors are.

DEFENSE

King cobras are long, strong, and **venomous**.
So what do they have to fear? Adult cobras face
danger from mongooses. These mammals are quick
enough to bite cobras before the snakes can bite
them! Young king cobras must watch out for army
ants, civet cats, and giant centipedes.

The king cobra is famous for the way it defends
itself. When threatened, it raises up its body and
makes a growl-like hissing noise. It also flattens its
neck to form a hood. From this position, a king
cobra is ready to strike. It has good aim. And, one
bite can release enough venom to kill 20 people!

Many people fear deadly king cobras. However,
these snakes avoid humans whenever possible.
Still, humans pose a threat to the king cobra's

survival. The snakes face **habitat** destruction.
Humans also capture them for their skin and for
use in medicines.

Even elephants are scared of a cobra's threatening stance!

FOOD

The king cobra's main source of food is other snakes. King cobras even eat **venomous** snakes, including other cobras! They swallow their food whole, and snakes are the perfect shape. Cobras also eat lizards, eggs, and small mammals if necessary.

King cobras actively hunt their prey. Once they find it, they rear up and bite down. As they bite, strong muscles squeeze their venom glands. The venom travels through the cobra's short, sharp fangs at the front of the jaws.

The venom enters the prey and kills it quickly. This poison also begins to **digest** the food for the cobra.

A snake can still breathe while swallowing a big meal. The opening of its windpipe moves forward to allow this.

BABIES

King cobras breed between January and April. Afterward, the female snake lays 20 to 40 eggs. The number of eggs depends on her size.

Lots of snakes lay eggs. But, king cobras are the only snakes that build nests for them. The female uses her body and head to scrape together leaves, grass, and other materials. This is where she lays her eggs. She covers them with more leaves and then lies on top of them.

The nest helps control the temperature of the eggs. The eggs **incubate** for 65 to 80 days. During this time, both the male and female king cobras guard the nest.

When the babies hatch, they are already 18 to 20 inches (46 to 51 cm) long. Soon, these growing snakes **shed** for the first time. As the snakes age, they will do this every time their skin gets too small or worn. King cobras live for about 20 years.

A baby king cobra's venom is already full strength.

GLOSSARY

digest - to break down food into simpler substances the body can absorb.

Elapidae (uh-LAP-uh-dee) - the scientific name for the elapid family. This family includes poisonous snakes such as cobras, mambas, sea snakes, taipans, and kraits.

external - of, relating to, or being on the outside.

habitat - a place where a living thing is naturally found.

incubate - to keep eggs warm so they will hatch.

organ - a part of an animal or a plant composed of several kinds of tissues. An organ performs a specific function. The heart, liver, gallbladder, and intestines are organs of an animal.

plain - a flat or rolling stretch of land without trees.

sea level - the level of the ocean's surface. Land
elevations and sea depths are measured from sea level.

shed - to cast off hair, feathers, skin, or other coverings
or parts by a natural process.

venom - a poison produced by some animals and
insects. It usually enters a victim through a bite or a
sting. Something that produces venom is venomous.

WEB SITES

To learn more about king cobras, visit ABDO
Publishing Company on the World Wide Web at
www.abdopublishing.com. Web sites about king
cobras are featured on our Book Links page. These
links are routinely monitored and updated to provide
the most current information available.

INDEX

A

Asia 12

B

babies 20
belly 9
body 4, 6, 8, 9, 16,
   20

C

cold-blooded 4
color 8, 9

D

defense 4, 6, 16

E

ears 14
eggs 20
Elapidae (family) 5

F

fangs 4, 18
food 10, 14, 18

H

habitat 4, 8, 10,
   12, 17
head 14, 20
hood 4, 9, 16

J

Jacobson's organ
   15
jaws 14, 18

L

life span 21

M

mouth 15

N

nests 20
nostrils 14

O

Ophiophagus
   (genus) 5

S

scales 4
senses 14, 15
shedding 21
size 4, 6, 12, 16, 20
skin 4, 17, 21

T

tail 9
threats 14, 16, 17
tongue 14, 15

V

venom 4, 6, 16, 18
vertebrates 4
vibrations 14